MRT-DOF

Department of Economic and Social Affairs
Population Division

ST/ESA/SER.A/181

Population Growth, Structure and Distribution

The Concise Report

 United Nations   New York, 1999

NOTE

The designations employed and the presentation of the material in the publication do not imply the expression of any opinion whatsoever on the part of the Secretariat of the United Nations concerning the legal status of any country, territory, city or area or of its authorities, or concerning the delimitation of its frontiers or boundaries.

The term "country" as used in the text of this publication also refers, as appropriate, to territories or areas.

The designations "more developed" and "less developed" regions are intended for statistical convenience and do not necessarily express a judgement about the stage reached by a particular country or area in the development process.

ST/ESA/SER.A/181

UNITED NATIONS PUBLICATION
Sales No. E.99.XIII.15
ISBN 92-1-151338-3

UN 2
ST/ESA/SER.A/181

PREFACE

The Economic and Social Council, in its resolution 1995/55 of 28 July 1995, endorsed the topic-oriented work programme of the Commission on Population and Development, under which the topic proposed for the deliberations at the 1999 session of the Commission was "Population growth, structure and distribution".[1] The subject was chosen to complement the topics for previous Commissions ("Reproductive rights and reproductive health" in 1996, "International migration and development" in 1997 and "Health and mortality" in 1998), so that the reports for 1996-1999, taken together, would provide a broad review of trends and policy issues in key areas covered in the Programme of Action of the International Conference on Population and Development,[2] and provide a foundation for the five-year review and appraisal of progress in implementation of the Programme of Action in 1999.[3]

As requested by the Council, the Population Division, Department of Economic and Social Affairs of the United Nations Secretariat, annually prepares the world population monitoring report on the topic of each annual session of the Commission. The full report is accompanied by a summarized version, the "concise report". Each of these reports is presented and discussed at the Commission and then revised for publication. *Population Growth, Structure and Distribution: The Concise Report* is the revised version of the concise report on world population monitoring for 1999.[4]

The *Concise Report* was prepared by the Population Division. Acknowledgement is due to the United Nations Statistics Division for the preparation of the annex on data collection, data availability and data quality.

---

[1]*See Official Records of the Economic and Social Council, 1995, Supplement No. 7* (E/1995/27), annex I, sect. III, para. 3.
[2]*Report of the International Conference on Population and Development, Cairo, 5-13 September 1994* (United Nations publication, Sales No. E.95.XIII.18), chap. I, resolution 1, annex.
[3]See ESA/P/WP.18; and E/CN.9/1999/PC/2.
[4]See E/CN.9/1999/2.

CONTENTS

Explanatory notes

Symbols of United Nations documents are composed of capital letters combined with figures.

Various symbols have been used in the tables throughout this report, as follows:

Two dots (..) indicate that data are not available or are not separately reported.

An em dash (—) indicates that the amount is nil or negligible.

A hyphen (-) indicates that the item is not applicable.

A minus sign (-) before a figure indicates a decrease.

A full stop (.) is used to indicate decimals.

A slash (/) indicates a crop year or financial year, for example, 1994/95.

Use of a hyphen (-) between years, for example, 1994-1995, signifies the full period involved, including the beginning and end years.

Reference to dollars ($) indicates United States dollars, unless otherwise stated.

Details and percentages in tables do not necessarily add to totals because of rounding.

The term "billion" signifies a thousand million.

The group of least developed countries currently comprises 48 countries: Afghanistan, Angola, Bangladesh, Benin, Bhutan, Burkina Faso, Burundi, Cambodia, Cape Verde, the Central African Republic, Chad, the Comoros, the Democratic Republic of the Congo, Djibouti, Equatorial Guinea, Eritrea, Ethiopia, the Gambia, Guinea, Guinea-Bissau, Haiti, Kiribati, the Lao People's Democratic Republic, Lesotho, Liberia, Madagascar, Malawi, Maldives, Mali, Mauritania, Mozambique, Myanmar, Nepal, the Niger, Rwanda, Samoa, Sao Tome and Principe, Sierra Leone, Solomon Islands, Somalia, the Sudan, Togo, Tuvalu, Uganda, the United Republic of Tanzania, Vanuatu, Yemen and Zambia.

INTRODUCTION

The second half of the twentieth century is demographically unprecedented. This is especially the case for the quarter-century since the 1974 United Nations World Population Conference at Bucharest. World population size has increased from 4 billion persons in 1974 to nearly 6 billion today. At the same time, the world population growth rate has fallen from about 2 per cent per year in 1970-1975 to 1.3 per cent today, the average number of children per couple has fallen from 4.5 to 2.7 and life expectancy at birth has risen from 58 years to 65 years. The share of the world's population living in urban areas has increased from 36 to 47 per cent and the number of mega-cities of 10 million persons or more has multiplied from 5 to 18. The number of persons who have moved to another country has risen to over 125 million today.

The demographic transition (that is to say, the transition from high to low birth and death rates) has not proceeded uniformly in all countries. In 1974, the transition was well under way or nearly completed in many countries and had barely begun in others. Although in 1998 this transition has occurred or is occurring in nearly every country, the timing and pace of the transition vary; and in some regions and countries, steps backward are occurring. For example, acquired immunodeficiency syndrome (AIDS) and other emerging diseases in some countries and economic and political dislocations in others have reversed past progress in improving health and reducing mortality.

The consequences of population growth for the pace of economic development have been a matter of vigorous and contentious debate. The impacts of rapid population growth have varied considerably by country and over time. Nonetheless, a general view remains that the rapid population growth of many developing countries makes it more difficult for these countries to achieve improvements in the standard of living as well as to protect their environments.

The Programme of Action of the International Conference on Population and Development reflected a consensus that slower population growth bought more time for Governments to adjust. However, the slowing population growth does not itself ensure that favourable policy and institutional changes will occur. Economic and demographic change are mutually interacting forces influenced by institutional settings and Government policy. As a result, population policies are an important element of the policy-making components needed to advance economic development, eliminate poverty and foster long-run environmental stewardship.

Population Growth, Structure and Distribution: The Concise Report reviews the demographic changes in population size and growth in the world and its urban and rural areas; the changes in mortality, fertility and migration that underlie these changes; and the population policies that Governments have adopted in response to their concerns with national aspects of population and

1

development. The *Concise Report* concludes with a review of the state of knowledge on the interrelationships of population with poverty, food and the environment.

Understanding demographic change and its interrelationships with development needs to be based on timely and high-quality data. An annex to the *Concise Report* summarizes the state of data collection around the world and stresses that more Government commitment, particularly more resources for data collection and analysis, are needed to ensure that policies and programmes are effectively targeted, devised and reliably monitored.

I. POPULATION GROWTH AND ITS COMPONENTS

POPULATION GROWTH

The current world population size is the result of a historically short and unprecedented period of accelerated population growth (see table 1). Before the twentieth century, world population grew only slowly, if at all. Historical estimates (United Nations, 1973) suggest, for instance, that world population in 1750 was about 791 million people, with annual population growth rates still below half a per cent. Moderate population growth (below 0.6 per cent per year) prevailed during the rest of the eighteenth century and throughout the nineteenth century. Accelerated population growth, with growth rates passing the 1 per cent mark in the 1920s and ultimately peaking at 2.04 per cent in the late 1960s, is clearly a phenomenon of the twentieth century.

The accelerating pace of population growth can be illustrated by the time that it took to add one billion people to the world population. From 1804, when the world passed the 1 billion mark, it took 123 years to reach 2 billion people, 33 years to add another billion people to reach 3 billion people in 1960, 14 years to reach 4 billion, and just 13 years to achieve 5 billion in 1987. It is estimated that the 6 billion people mark will be passed in 1999, after only 12 years of continued population growth.

In 1998, the world population stood at 5.9 billion persons, growing at a rate of 1.3 per cent annually and increasing by about 78 million persons every year. About 96 per cent of the total annual population increase occurs in the less developed regions. According to the United Nations official population estimates and projections, the world population in 2050 will be in the range of 7.3 billion to 10.7 billion persons (see fig. I). In the medium-fertility variant projection, which is often considered the most likely, world population will stand at 8.9 billion persons in 2050 (United Nations, 1999a).

As a result of marked differences in growth patterns by level of development, the proportion of people living in the more developed regions has declined and is projected to continue declining through the first part of the twenty-first century. Thus, while in 1970 about one quarter of the world population lived in the more developed regions, by 1998 that proportion had dropped to one fifth, and according to the medium-fertility variant just 13 per cent of the world population will reside in the more developed regions in 2050.

Population distribution and population growth differ markedly among the major areas, past and present. Asia, Africa, and Latin America and the Caribbean all increased their share of the world population between 1970 and 1998. The Asian share of the world population rose from 58 to 61 per cent, the African share from 10 to 13 per cent, and the Latin America and the Caribbean share

TABLE 1. POPULATION OF THE WORLD AND ITS MAJOR AREAS, 1750-2050

Major area	1750	1800	1850	1900	1950	1970	1998	2050
A. Population size (millions)								
World total	791	978	1 262	1 650	2 521	3 696	5 901	8 909
Africa	106	107	111	133	221	357	749	1 766
Asia	502	635	809	947	1 402	2 147	3 585	5 268
Europe	163	203	276	408	547	656	729	628
Latin America and the Caribbean	16	24	38	74	167	285	504	809
Northern America	2	7	26	82	172	232	305	392
Oceania	2	2	2	6	13	19	30	46
B. Percentage distribution								
World total	100	100	100	100	100	100	100	100
Africa	13.4	10.9	8.8	8.1	8.8	9.7	12.7	19.8
Asia	63.5	64.9	64.1	57.4	55.6	58.1	60.8	59.1
Europe	20.6	20.8	21.9	24.7	21.7	17.8	12.4	7.0
Latin America and the Caribbean	2.0	2.5	3.0	4.5	6.6	7.7	8.5	9.1
Northern America	0.3	0.7	2.1	5.0	6.8	6.3	5.2	4.4
Oceania	0.3	0.2	0.2	0.4	0.5	0.5	0.5	0.5

Source: Population Division, Department of Economic and Social Affairs of the United Nations Secretariat, *World Population Prospects: The 1998 Revision*, vol. I, *Comprehensive Tables* (United Nations publication, Sales No. E.99.XIII.9).

4

Figure I. World population size: past estimates and medium-, high- and low-fertility variants, 1950-2050

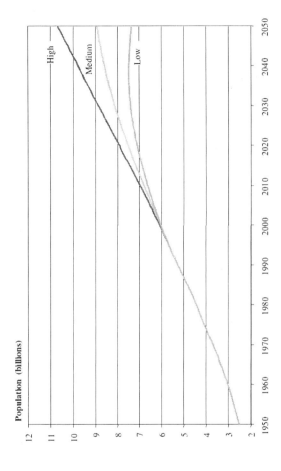

Population (billions)

Source: Population Division, Department of Economic and Social Affairs of the United Nations Secretariat, *World Population Prospects: The 1998 Revision*, vol. I, *Comprehensive Tables* (United Nations publication, Sales No. E.99.XIII.9).

5

from 8 to 9 per cent (see table 1). During the same period, the share of Northern America declined from 6 to 5 per cent, and that of Europe from 18 to 12 per cent.

Most major areas are currently exhibiting population growth rates well above 1 per cent: Africa is growing annually by 2.4 per cent, followed by Latin America and the Caribbean (1.6 per cent), Asia (1.4 per cent) and Oceania (1.3 per cent). Only Northern America, with 0.85 per cent, and Europe, with 0.03 per cent, exhibit growth under one per cent per year. Accordingly, and also depending on their current population size, each major area's contribution to global population growth differs widely. The most populous and the fastest growing major areas are the main contributors to world population growth: of the 78 million persons added each year to the world population during the period 1995-2000, 63 per cent (49 million) are from Asia and 23 per cent (17 million) from Africa. Latin America and the Caribbean currently adds less than 8 million people annually to world population growth (about 10 per cent of the total increment), followed by Northern America, with 2.6 million or 3 per cent of the annual global increase. The annual contributions of Oceania (about 381,000) and Europe (about 195,000) are very small.

Annual population growth rates vary widely among countries, from negative growth among some Eastern European countries to very high growth rates among some African and Asian countries. Altogether, there are 24 countries, constituting 1.7 per cent of the world population, that exhibit average annual growth rates of 3 per cent or more. At the other end of the spectrum, 24 countries, with 6.1 per cent of the global population, have declining populations. Two thirds of the world population lives in the 88 countries that exhibit annual growth rates ranging between 0.5 and 2 per cent.

The number of countries with 100 million or more inhabitants has increased rapidly, rising from 4 countries in 1950 to 10 countries in 1998 (see table 2). By 2050, according to the medium-fertility projection variant, there will be 18 such countries. In 1998, China, with 1.26 billion inhabitants, was the country with the largest population in the world, followed by India with 982 million. The third, fourth and fifth most populous countries were the United States of America (274 million), Indonesia (206 million) and Brazil (166 million). According to the United Nations medium-fertility projection variant, India is expected to be the largest country in the world in 2050 with 1.53 billion inhabitants, followed by China (1.48 billion), the United States (349 million), Pakistan (345 million) and Indonesia (312 million).

FERTILITY

Over the past three decades, substantial declines in fertility have taken place in all areas of the world. Since 1970-1975, world total fertility has declined by 39 per cent from 4.5 births per woman to the current level of 2.7 births per woman. In the less developed regions, women are currently having more than two fewer children than women did three decades ago. The average number of births per woman in the less developed regions declined by 45 per cent from 5.4 during 1970-1975 to 3.0 in 1995-2000. In the more developed regions, fertility declined from 2.1 births per woman during 1970-1975 to a

TABLE 2.   COUNTRIES WITH A POPULATION OF OVER 100 MILLION
IN 1950, 1998 AND 2050

Rank	Country	Population (millions)
1950		
1	China	555
2	India	358
3	United States of America	158
4	Russian Federation	102
1998		
1	China	1 256
2	India	982
3	United States of America	274
4	Indonesia	206
5	Brazil	166
6	Pakistan	148
7	Russian Federation	147
8	Japan	128
9	Bangladesh	125
10	Nigeria	106
2050		
1	India	1 529
2	China	1 478
3	United States of America	349
4	Pakistan	345
5	Indonesia	312
6	Nigeria	244
7	Brazil	244
8	Bangladesh	212
9	Ethiopia	169
10	Democratic Republic of the Congo	160
11	Mexico	147
12	Philippines	131
13	Viet Nam	127
14	Russian Federation	121
15	Iran (Islamic Republic of)	115
16	Egypt	115
17	Japan	105
18	Turkey	101

Source: Population Division, Department of Economic and Social Affairs of the United Nations Secretariat, *World Population Prospects: The 1998 Revision*, vol. I, *Comprehensive Tables* (United Nations publication, Sales No. E.99.XIII.9).

historical low of 1.6 for the current period, 1995-2000. Even though fertility has declined to relatively moderate levels in many developing countries and to below replacement level in some, a large number of live births are occurring annually owing to the continued growth in the number of women of childbearing age, a legacy of past high-fertility levels. In the less developed regions, the average number of births per year was 104 million in 1970-1975; the annual number has grown to 117 million births today.

Variations in fertility among the major areas of the world persist. Total fertility rates range from 1.4 and 1.9 births per woman in Europe and Northern America, respectively, to 5.1 in Africa. Rates for Asia and Latin America and the Caribbean fall in between, at 2.6 and 2.7 births per woman, respectively. Analysis of trends in fertility for 184 countries shows that in 1970-1975, 79 countries exhibited fertility levels greater than six children per woman, whereas 16 countries had fertility below the replacement level of 2.1 births per woman. By 1995-2000, the number of high-fertility countries was down to 20 and the number below replacement had increased to 58, demonstrating a shift towards lower fertility in all parts of the world (see table 3). Indeed, the data show that as many as 60 countries began their fertility transition as of 1970-1975, nearly half those countries (28) being in Africa, 19 in Asia, and 9 in Latin America and the Caribbean. Even among countries that exhibited low fertility 30 years ago, rates have continued to decline. In 22 countries of Europe and Northern America, the current fertility rate is 1.5 births per woman or below. Bulgaria, Italy, the Czech Republic, Romania and Spain have an average of just 1.2 births per woman in 1995-2000, while in the Russian Federation, Germany, Estonia, Greece, Slovenia and Latvia, the average total fertility rate is 1.3 births per woman. Fertility, nevertheless, remains high in many countries. For example, total fertility is still above 6.5 births per woman in 10 countries or areas, namely, Afghanistan, Angola, Burkina Faso, the Gaza Strip, Malawi, Mali, the Niger, Somalia, Uganda and Yemen.

Even though there is a broad agreement about conditions that favour the onset of the fertility transition, there is no consensus regarding specific conditions that need to be present for the transition to begin. It is possible, however, to discern the commonalities among groups of countries, commonalities that are related to factors associated with the fertility decline, such as socioeconomic development, decline in mortality levels, female education, urbanization and family planning programmes (Kirk, 1996; Mason, 1992).

Several commonalities are apparent. For instance, all but 2 of the 20 high-fertility countries in 1995-2000 are classified by the United Nations as least developed countries and most of them are less urbanized. In most of these countries, infant and under-five mortality levels are still very high. In the 17 sub-Saharan African countries of the group, little or no change has occurred in levels of infant mortality since the 1970s and current levels are well over 100 deaths per 1,000 live births (United Nations, 1998a and 1999a). The rate of use of any type of contraception to limit or space births is less than 10 per cent in most of the 14 countries for which information is available (United Nations, 1996); gross secondary school enrolment ratios among females are below 10 in most of the 20 high-fertility countries (UNICEF, 1998); and the incidence of

8

early marriage continues to be high in almost all current high-fertility countries (United Nations, 1990).

TABLE 3. DISTRIBUTION OF COUNTRIES ACCORDING TO LEVEL OF TOTAL
FERTILITY RATE IN 1970-1975 AND 1995-2000, BY MAJOR AREA

Total fertility rate	Africa	Asia	Latin America and the Caribbean	Oceania	Europe and Northern America	Total
			1970-1975			
6.0 and over	44	22	9	4	0	79
5.0-5.9	5	13	6	1	0	25
4.0-4.9	2	6	7	3	1	19
3.0-3.9	2	4	7	0	2	15
2.1-2.9	0	5	2	2	21	30
Less than 2.1	0	0	0	0	16	16
	53	50	31	10	40	184
			1995-2000			
6.0 and over	17	3	0	0	0	20
5.0-5.9	17	7	0	0	0	24
4.0-4.9	9	6	6	4	0	25
3.0-3.9	7	9	5	1	0	22
2.1-2.9	2	13	15	3	2	35
Less than 2.1	1	12	5	2	38	58
	53	50	31	10	40	184

Source: Population Division, Department of Economic and Social Affairs of the United Nations Secretariat, *World Population Prospects: The 1998 Revision*, vol. I, *Comprehensive Tables* (United Nations publication, Sales No. E.99.XIII.9).

In countries where fertility transition has been under way since 1970-1975, a significant increase in contraceptive prevalence was an important factor in fertility decline. In Morocco, Tunisia and Algeria, the percentage of married women using contraception ranges from 40 to 50 per cent, up from 20 to 30 per cent in the early 1980s. Significant increases in contraceptive prevalence were also evident in Botswana and Lesotho in Southern Africa, and Kenya and Zimbabwe in Eastern Africa (United Nations, 1996). In Asia, although data on contraceptive use is not available for all countries, the data for Bangladesh, Jordan, the Islamic Republic of Iran and Nepal indicate that increased contraceptive prevalence might have played a role in fertility decline. In Latin America and the Caribbean, where all the high-fertility countries in 1970-1975 experienced rapid declines in fertility, almost all the decline in fertility can be attributed to increased use of contraception (Chackiel and Schkolnik, 1997; United Nations, 1996).

9

The other commonalities among countries in transition—that is, countries where fertility transition has been under way since 1970-1975—include the decline in levels of child mortality since the 1970s, increased levels of education among women and changing marriage patterns, in particular a rise in age at marriage. In Algeria, Botswana, Kenya, Lesotho, Morocco, Tunisia and Zimbabwe, strong declines in infant and under-five mortality have occurred since the 1970s (United Nations, 1998a). Education of women—as measured by the mean number of years of schooling completed among respondents in the Demographic and Health Surveys—is highest in Zimbabwe, Botswana and Kenya, but oddly, education of women in the Northern African countries of Morocco and Egypt is well below the levels for the former three countries. In Asia, recent rises in the age at marriage has been a major factor accounting for the rapid decline in fertility in the 15 countries that have initiated their fertility transition since 1970-1975. In Pakistan, for example, the percentage of 15- to 19-year-old women who were married was 73 per cent prior to 1970 but had decreased to 31 per cent for a more recent cohort of 15- to 19-year-olds. Similar though not as dramatic declines in the proportions among married 15- to 19-year-old women were also seen in Nepal, the Syrian Arab Republic, Kuwait, the United Arab Emirates and Qatar (United Nations, 1990; United Arab Emirates, 1991; Qatar, 1991). On the other hand, changes in marriage patterns accounted for little of the fertility decline observed in Latin America and the Caribbean in the 1970s, 1980s and 1990s (Chackiel and Schkolnik, 1997).

Each of the commonalities identified above is not always autonomously conducive to fertility decline, nor are they always collectively associated with changes in fertility levels. For example, in Bangladesh, a least developed country—but with effective family-planning activities—fertility declined from 7.0 births per woman in 1970-1975 to just 3.1 in 1995-2000 despite slow economic and social progress (Cleland and others, 1994). On the other hand, several Arab countries in Western Asia, such as Jordan, Saudi Arabia and Oman, lead the indicators of economic wealth although their fertility levels have shown little decline over the past 30 years. In addition, large variations in mortality levels can be found among countries with high fertility. In Jordan, Saudi Arabia (total fertility rate of 5.1 and 5.9, respectively) and Oman (total fertility rate of 7.2) infant mortality levels for the period 1995-2000 were 30, 23 and 25 deaths per 1,000 live births, respectively (United Nations, 1999a).

In the post-transition countries, where fertility is increasingly becoming lower and old postulates of transition theory becoming less and less pertinent, increasing attention is being paid to the determinants of post-transition fertility as more countries enter this phase. The increased status of women appears to be one of the important determinants of continued low fertility. There is some evidence, however, that several factors that have traditionally been negatively associated with fertility levels may now play an opposite role under modern conditions. For example, economic well-being and education have conventionally been negatively associated with fertility. Yet recent trends in Sweden suggest the opposite (United Nations, 1998b). However, given the diversity of post-transition countries, research into the determinants of fertility in different low-fertility settings is clearly called for.

At the global level, the continuing progress in the reduction of mortality achieved in the last quarter of the twentieth century is remarkable. This is revealed in the increase in the level of life expectancy at birth from 58 years prior to the 1974 United Nations World Population Conference at Bucharest to 65 years today (see fig. II). Simultaneously, infant mortality has declined from 93 deaths per 1,000 live births to 57 today.

In 35 of 43 countries from the more developed regions with a population of 150,000 or more in 1995, life expectancy currently exceeds 70 years; in 24 of them, it is higher than 75 years. In the first half of the twentieth century, mortality improvements were concentrated in childhood and the working ages, whereas mortality decreases at older ages were slow. Since 1950 and especially after 1970, the pace of mortality improvements at older ages has been accelerating in most developed countries with established market economies. As a result, in developed market economy countries, the number of persons surviving to very advanced ages had risen markedly.

Estimates for 1995-2000 show that among the less developed regions, Latin America and the Caribbean as a whole has the highest life expectancy (69.2 years), having experienced an increase of 8.3 years since 1970-1975. Six countries have a life expectancy of more than 75 years, similar to that of developed market economy countries. However, life expectancy is lower than 70 years in a group of 10 Latin American and Caribbean countries, including Brazil, which is the most populous country of the area.

Mortality decline was also impressive in Eastern Asia and Western Asia, where regional life expectancies currently average 71.0 and 68.0 years, respectively. The progress was slower in South-eastern Asia (life expectancy of 65.7 years) and South-central Asia (62.3 years). However, some countries have much higher mortality levels than their neighbours; for instance, life expectancy is only 45.5 years in Afghanistan, 47.5 years in East Timor and 53 years in Cambodia.

In Africa, mortality is even higher and the speed of improvements is particularly slow. Only in Northern Africa did life expectancy increase considerably, and its current level of 64.8 years is higher than the year 2000 goal. In the other four African regions, life expectancy is substantially lower than 60 years—in Southern Africa by 5.6 years, in Middle Africa by 9.9 years, in Western Africa by 10.1 years and in Eastern Africa by 14.6 years.

As a result of uneven mortality trends, international variations in life expectancy have become even more pronounced than they were a generation ago. In 1970-1975, the gap in life expectancy between the highest level of 74.4 years recorded in Norway and the lowest level of 38.0 years estimated for Afghanistan was 36.4 years or 96 per cent of the lowest level. By 1995-2000, the difference between Japan's life expectancy of 80.0 years and Sierra Leone's 37.2 years attained 42.8 years or 115 per cent of the lowest level.

The Programme of Action of the International Conference on Population and Development calls for an increase of life expectancy at birth to 70 years or more by the year 2005 in countries that have today moderate or low mortality

Figure II. Life expectancy at birth, 1995-2000
(Both sexes)

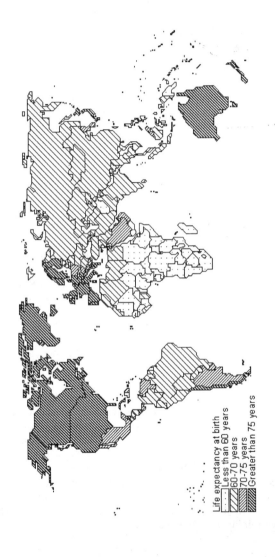

Life expectancy at birth
Less than 60 years
60-70 years
70-75 years
Greater than 75 years

NOTE: Estimates are not presented for countries or areas with population under 150,000.
Source: Population Division, Department of Economic and Social Affairs of the United Nations Secretariat, *World Population Prospects: The 1998 Revision*, vol. I, *Comprehensive Tables* (United Nations publication, Sales No. E.99.XIII.9).

levels, and for an increase to at least 65 years in countries with the highest mortality levels. Should the mortality assumptions hold of *World Population Prospects: The 1998 Revision* (United Nations, 1999a, 1999b), the United Nations official world population estimates and projections, by 2005 life expectancy would still be lower than called for by the Programme of Action in 72 countries. In fact, in 54 countries with a combined population of 870 million, life expectancy would not have reached even the lower goal of 65 years.

The causes of recent mortality trends at the national level include a large array of factors. The medical and hygienic interventions to combat or prevent infectious and parasitic diseases were largely responsible for the rapid decreases in the prevalence of communicable disease and associated mortality declines, especially among children, that many developing countries have experienced since the 1960s. However, the war against communicable disease is not yet won. Globally, infectious and parasitic diseases, respiratory infections, malnutrition, and maternal and neonatal mortality account for more than 40 per cent of all deaths (World Health Organization, 1998).

Recent years have witnessed a devastating toll from human immunodeficiency syndrome/acquired immunodeficiency syndrome (HIV/AIDS) in a number of countries from all regions of the world (United Nations/Joint United Nations Programme on HIV/AIDS, 1999). However, more than 90 per cent of HIV cases have occurred in the developing countries. The epidemic has been particularly severe in sub-Saharan Africa. In the 29 most affected African countries, life expectancy at birth is currently seven years less than it would have been in the absence of HIV/AIDS. In the nine countries with an adult prevalence of HIV infection of 10 per cent or more, life expectancy is, on average, 10 years less than it would have been in the absence of HIV. In addition, the demographic impact of HIV/AIDS is expected to intensify in the short-term future. Thus, by 2010-2015, those nine countries will see their life expectancy reduced by an estimated 16 years because of the impact of the disease.

Botswana and Zimbabwe are the two countries most affected by HIV/AIDS, with an adult prevalence of about 22 per cent each. As a result of the epidemic, life expectancy at birth in Botswana has dropped from 61 years in 1990-1995 to 47 years in 1995-2000, and it is expected to decline further to 41 years by 2000-2005. In Zimbabwe, life expectancy at birth fell to 52 years in 1990-1995, and is expected to be just 44 years in 1995-2000 and 41 years in 2000-2005. Another highly affected country is South Africa, where the epidemic started later than in Zimbabwe and one of every eight adults was infected by HIV in 1997. Owing to the later start of the epidemic in South Africa, the major demographic impact of the disease is yet to come. In 1990-1995, life expectancy at birth (estimated at 59 years) had been barely affected by the epidemic, but current projections indicate that by 2005-2010 life expectancy at birth might fall below 45 years.

In many of the more developed countries, decreasing mortality from cardiovascular disease and neoplasms was made possible during the past two or three decades by advances in medical treatment and beneficial changes in lifestyles. Such gains, however, have not been made by some countries of Eastern Europe, which have experienced a stagnation of mortality or even increases in mortality rates at adult ages, particularly among men. Rising mortality because of non-medical causes, including accidents, injuries and violent deaths, has also contributed to this trend.

INTERNATIONAL MIGRATION

During the twentieth century, the contribution of net migration to population growth has been of minor demographic importance for most countries, especially those where natural increase has been high. However, the marked reduction of fertility experienced by a growing number of countries over the past three decades means that the role of international migration in determining population growth has been rising. For developed countries in particular, the low levels of fertility that have prevailed over recent periods means that moderate or even low levels of international migration have had a significant impact on population growth. Estimates derived from *World Population Prospects: The 1998 Revision* indicate that during 1970-1995 the Western market economy countries absorbed 35 million migrants in net terms, accounting for 28 per cent of their combined population growth. In contrast, the loss of those 35 million migrants reduced population growth in the rest of the world by under 2 per cent.

Net migration for most countries amounted to a low percentage of natural increase: in 54 per cent of all countries, net migration raised or lowered natural increase by 12 per cent or less. However, in 15 countries net migration lowered natural increase by four fifths or more, and in 24 countries net migration raised natural increase by one third or more. Countries or areas where net migration contributed to raising population growth by a sizeable percentage of natural increase were of two types: (*a*) countries with relatively small populations and moderate to high rates of natural increase; and (*b*) countries with very low rates of natural increase. Both types tend to be characterized by having fostered the admission of international migrants since 1970. They include the main traditional countries of immigration, many of the European market economy countries and the oil-exporting countries of Western Asia.

Given the large economic and demographic disparities existing between developed and developing countries, it has been argued that migration from developing to developed countries will necessarily rise as developing countries become increasingly incapable of absorbing the large increases expected in the labour force (Emmerij, 1993; Golini, Righi and Bonifazi, 1993). Since such disparities have been very much in evidence during 1970-1995, it is instructive to consider whether the experience of the past in some way validates such expectations.

It has been suggested that emigration tends to be higher where population growth rates are high. A comparison of natural increase and net migration by country indicates that the relation between the two may not be simple. The data show that although at very low levels of natural increase (below 0.5 per cent) countries appear more likely to experience immigration rather than emigration, at high levels of natural increase (above 2 per cent) there are numerous countries experiencing either net immigration or net emigration. The analysis

14

suggests that rapid rates of population growth do not on their own necessarily lead to increased emigration.

Migration has always been an important process leading to the redistribution of population. At the beginning of the twentieth century, it was a major component of the population growth of the relatively sparsely populated countries of overseas European expansion. By the end of the century, international migration has become a key component of the population growth of most of the highly developed market economy countries of Europe, and has remained an important determinant of population growth in Northern America and Australia. From the perspective of a world divided into a developing "South" and a developed "North", international migration is often seen as the main process leading to the redistribution of population. When very low levels of natural increase are achieved and sustained, international migration can indeed play a role in affecting population growth, but it too would need to be sustained. Unless net migration increases exponentially, it cannot counterbalance over the long run the effects of either a positive or a negative rate of natural increase (Keyfitz, 1971; Espenshade, Bouvier and Arthur, 1982), and at least during the twentieth century no major region has experienced anything akin to an exponential growth in net migration over a prolonged period.

GOVERNMENT VIEWS AND POPULATION POLICIES

Continued high rates of population growth remain an issue of policy concern for many countries of the world, although fewer countries are now expressing a concern than at the time of the 1994 International Conference on Population and Development. In fact, in response to low levels of fertility in a growing number of countries and the social and economic consequences of the resultant population ageing, more countries are expressing concern about their low rates of population growth. The proportion of Governments that consider their rate of population growth to be too high declined from 44 per cent in 1993 to 41 per cent in 1998. In parallel, the proportion of Governments perceiving their growth rate to be too low increased from 11 per cent in 1993 to 14 per cent in 1998 (see table 4).

Most of the countries that express the view that their rates of population growth are too high are in the less developed regions. Countries that view their

TABLE 4. GOVERNMENTS' VIEWS OF POPULATION GROWTH RATE, 1974-1998
(*Percentage of countries*)

Year	Too high	Satisfactory	Too low	Total	Number of countries
1974	27.6	47.4	25.0	100.0	156
1983	36.3	45.2	18.5	100.0	168
1993	43.7	45.3	11.0	100.0	190
1998	41.1	44.4	14.5	100.0	180

Source: Population policy data bank maintained by the Population Division, Department of Economic and Social Affairs of the United Nations Secretariat.

15

population growth as satisfactory include most of the developed countries, as well as a majority of countries in South America and a few countries in Africa and Western Asia. Countries that view their population growth as too low are located primarily in Eastern Europe and Western Asia, with a small number scattered in other regions. In 1998, the greatest shift in views with regard to population growth occurred among the countries of the former USSR and Eastern Europe. Many of these countries considered their population growth to be satisfactory in 1993 but by 1998 had shifted to the view of considering their population growth rates to be too low.

The proportion of Governments that have policies aimed at influencing population growth increased from 45 per cent in 1974 to 63 per cent in 1993. By 1998, this proportion had declined to 56 per cent. Seventy Governments (39 per cent) have policies aimed at lowering population growth, while 18 (10 per cent) have policies aimed at increasing population growth (see fig. III). In developing countries during the 15-year period from 1983 to 1998, the proportion of Governments intervening to influence population growth increased from 58 to 65 per cent. The proportion of Governments of developed countries intervening to influence population growth declined between 1983 and 1998 because a number of countries with policies to maintain or increase the rate of population growth shifted to a policy of non-intervention.

In Africa, an increasing number of countries are adopting population policies and intensifying efforts to reduce population growth. Similarly, in Asia a significant number of countries consider their population growth rates to be too high. In contrast, all countries of Eastern Asia view their population growth rates as satisfactory except China, which despite impressive results in reducing population growth has resumed viewing its population growth rate as too high. A number of countries in South-central Asia that earlier viewed the population growth rate as satisfactory perceived it in 1998 as too low and changed their policy of maintaining the growth rate to a policy of raising it. Of the 16 Governments of Western Asia whose views regarding population growth were known, six consider their growth rate to be too low and have a policy to increase it. In Latin America and the Caribbean, an increasing number of countries (62 per cent) consider their population growth rates to be satisfactory. A majority of the small, densely populated countries in the Caribbean and three countries in Central America consider population growth to be too high, whereas almost all countries in South America consider it to be satisfactory.

In Europe, an increasing number of countries are concerned with issues of declining fertility, declining population and ageing. In 1998, of the nine Governments of Eastern Europe whose views regarding population growth were known, seven considered it to be too low. Many of these Governments inaugurated policies to alter the current demographic situation and increase population growth. Among the 24 countries of Europe that have already responded to the Eighth United Nations Inquiry among Governments on Population and Development, nine (38 per cent) indicated that their goal was to raise fertility. In Oceania, both Australia and New Zealand remain satisfied with their population growth rates.

Figure III. Governments' policies on population growth rate, world, 1983-1998
(Percentage)

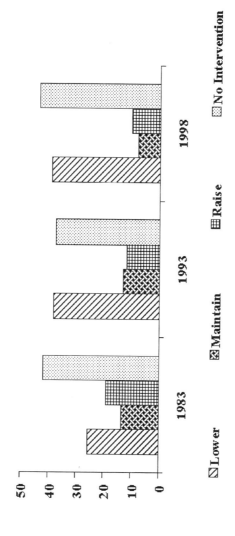

Source: Population policy data bank maintained by the Population Division, Department of Economic and Social Affairs of the United Nations Secretariat.

II. CHANGING POPULATION AGE STRUCTURES

An inevitable consequence of the demographic transition and the shift to lower fertility and mortality has been the evolution in population age structure. Developed countries have attained older age structures than were ever seen in the past, while developing countries are undergoing rapid shifts in respect of the share of children, youth and adults.

DEMOGRAPHIC ASPECTS

The world population under age 15 was estimated to be 1.79 billion in 1998. Among these children, 12 per cent lived in the more developed regions and 88 per cent in the less developed regions (see table 5). Between 1970 and 1998, the world child population increased from 1.39 to 1.79 billion, a 29 per cent increase. According to the United Nations' medium-fertility variant population projections, the number of children under age 15 in the world will grow only about two per cent more in the coming years, and after 2025 will decrease gradually to 1.75 billion in 2050, about the same number as today. In the less developed regions, the average annual growth rate of the child population was 1.6 per cent per year in the decade 1970-1980, but has slowed to an estimated 0.8 per cent per year for the decade of the 1990s. In the more developed regions, the number of children has already been declining since 1965.

Children aged under 15 currently make up 19 per cent of the population of the more developed regions, 33 per cent of that in the less developed regions, and 43 per cent in the least developed countries. All regions but Africa have experienced large declines in the percentage under age 15; in Africa the percentage declined only from 45 per cent to 43 per cent between 1970 and 1998. By 2050, children are projected to make up between 17 and 20 per cent of the population of most regions, but 14 per cent in Europe and 24 per cent in Africa.

Ages 15-24 represent a transition from childhood to adulthood in most societies. Many young men and women enter the labour force, marry and begin childbearing during this period of life. For society as a whole, rapid growth in the number of young people means a rapid growth in the demand for secondary and higher education, for jobs and for housing.

The world youth population aged 15-24 numbered 1.04 billion in 1998. By 2050, the youth population is projected to be 13 per cent larger than today, at 1.18 billion. Youth currently make up 18 per cent of the world population, ranging from 13 per cent of the population in Northern America and 14 per cent in Europe to 20 per cent in Africa and in Latin America and the Caribbean. Between 1998 and 2050, the growth rate of the world youth population is projected to slow, approaching a zero growth rate after 2010 for the world as a whole. However, in the least developed countries the youth population will continue to grow at over one per cent per year until after 2030. The population share of the age group 15-24 in the total population is projected to decrease between 1998 and 2050, from 14 to 11 per cent in the more developed regions, from 19 to 14 per cent in the less developed regions and from 20 to 17 per cent in the least developed countries.

TABLE 5. ESTIMATED AND PROJECTED REGIONAL DISTRIBUTION OF THE POPULATION AGED UNDER 15 YEARS AND THE POPULATION AGED 60 YEARS OR OVER—1970, 1998 AND 2050
(*Percentage*)

Region	Under age 15			Aged 60 or over		
	1970	1998	2050	1970	1998	2050
World total	100	100	100	100	100	100
More developed regions . . .	19	12	10	47	39	19
Less developed regions. . . .	81	88	90	53	61	81
Least developed countries .	10	15	20	5	5	9
Africa	12	18	24	6	6	11
Asia	63	61	57	45	53	63
Eastern Asia	27	20	15	23	27	26
China.	24	18	14	18	21	22
South-eastern Asia	9	9	9	5	6	9
South-central Asia	24	29	28	15	17	25
India	16	19	17	11	13	16
Western Asia	3	4	5	2	2	3
Europe.	12	7	5	33	25	11
Latin America and the Caribbean.	9	9	9	6	7	9
Northern America	5	4	4	10	9	6
Oceania	0.4	0.4	0.5	1	1	1

Source: Population Division, Department of Economic and Social Affairs of the United Nations Secretariat, *World Population Prospects: The 1998 Revision,* vol. II, *The Sex and Age Distribution of the World Populations: Medium Variant Projections* (United Nations publication, Sales No. E.99.XIII.8).

The world population of older persons is considerably smaller than the child population, but the older population is growing at a much faster rate. The number of persons aged 60 years or over is estimated to be 580 million in 1998. By 2050, it is projected to be more than three times as large, nearly 2 billion, at which time it will be larger than the world child population. The growth of the older population often receives attention in connection with the developed countries. However, the older population is increasing at a substantially faster rate in the less developed than the more developed regions.

Persons aged 60 or over currently make up 10 per cent of the world population. The percentage is much higher in the more developed regions (19 per cent) than in the less developed regions (8 per cent). It is especially low in the least developed countries (5 per cent). Among individual countries, the highest percentages are currently found in Italy (24 per cent) and Greece (23 per cent). Many other European countries, as well as Japan, have proportions nearly as high. By 2050, the older ages will make up a projected 22 per cent of the world population—33 per cent in the more developed regions, 21 per cent in the less developed regions, and 12 per cent in the least developed countries.

The oldest old, persons aged 80 years or more, currently number 66 million. They make up about 1 per cent of the world's population and 3 per cent of the population of the more developed regions. This oldest age group is, however, growing even faster than the older population as a whole. By 2050, the number of the oldest old is projected to be 5.6 times as large as at present. By that date, the oldest old will be 4 per cent of the total world population, and in the more developed regions one person out of 11 is projected to be aged 80 or more.

- It is necessary to look beyond 2050 to see the full consequences for population ageing of ongoing trends towards lower fertility and mortality rates. A range of alternative scenarios presented in the United Nations long-range population projections (United Nations, 1998c) show that future populations will reach a significantly older age structure than the populations of the present or even the populations of 2050. Figure IV shows projected trends in the proportion of the world population aged 60 or over through the year 2150 in the medium-fertility scenario, which assumes that all regions will have reached and will maintain replacement-level fertility after 2050, and that mortality rates will continue to improve. By 2150, persons aged 60 or over are projected to number 3.3 billion, nearly one person out of every three alive at that time. One in every 10 persons will be aged 80 or more. Only 18 per cent of the population will be a child aged under 15 years.

The regional composition of the older population is very different from that of the child population. In 1998, the more developed regions contained about two fifths of the world's older people but only one out of every eight children. By 2050, the more developed regions will contain less than one fifth of the world's older persons, for the older population is increasing at a substantially faster rate in the less developed than the more developed regions. Today, though, older persons make up a substantially higher proportion of the total population in the more developed than in the less developed regions. The "oldest" country in the world in 1998 was Italy, with 1.6 persons aged 60 years or older for each person under age 15, followed by Greece, Japan, Spain and Germany. By 2050, the oldest country will be Spain, with 3.6 persons aged 60 years or older for each person under age 15. Uganda is the world's youngest country, with 1 in every 31 persons aged 60 years or older in 1998.

Women outnumber men at the oldest ages. At ages 60 or over, there were an estimated 81 men for every 100 women globally in 1998, and at ages 80 or over there were only 53 men for every 100 women. This is because women are generally more likely to survive to older ages. The sex ratios of older age groups are lower in the more developed regions than in the less developed regions since there are larger differences in life expectancy between the sexes in the more developed regions. In addition, the sex ratio in the oldest age groups in the

Figure IV. Percentage of the world population under age 15, aged 60 years or over and aged 80 years or over, 1970-2050, medium-fertility variant

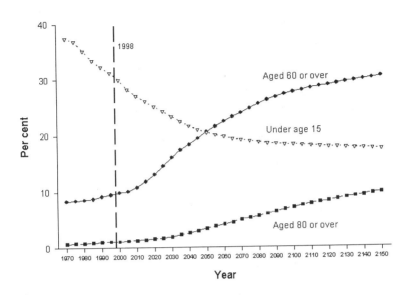

Source: Population Division, Department of Economic and Social Affairs of the United Nations Secretariat, *World Population Projections to 2150* (United Nations publication, Sales No. E.98.XIII.14).

more developed regions retains the effect of the heavy loss of men in the armed forces in some countries during the Second World War.

The relative deficit of men increases rapidly with rising age, after age 60. At ages 60-64, there are 94 men for each 100 women, at ages 80-84 there are 59, and at ages 90-94 only 36. There are estimated to be about four women for every man among the very small proportion who have survived beyond age 100.

Given the age patterns of the sex ratio, the rapid growth of the elderly population and the increase in the proportion in older age groups imply a decrease in the sex ratio for the total population and a greater increase in the number of older women than of older men. Projected increases between 1998 and 2050 in the number of persons aged 60 or over are 655 million for men and 753 million for women in the world as a whole. Projected increases during the same period in the number of persons aged 80 or over are 118 million for men and 184 million for women.

SOCIO-ECONOMIC ASPECTS

Changing age structure is likely to have wide-ranging economic and social consequences through such factors as economic growth, savings and investment, labour supply and employment, pension schemes, health and long-term care, intergenerational transfers, family composition and living arrangements. While once limited to developed countries, concern for ageing's consequences has spread to developing countries.

Because savings fuel economic growth, the relation between savings and ageing is an important policy issue. Savings rates peak at the end of working life and fall in retirement; however, the importance of this pattern for a nation's economic performance is unclear. Ageing's effects are transmitted through three channels: shrinking labour force, reduced household savings, and increased government pension and health expenditures. Evidence suggests that East Asia's rapid income growth is in part attributable to the rising size and share of the working age population (Asian Development Bank, 1997). The shrinking share of children led to fewer expenditures on children, inducing higher savings and investment. The studies show, however, that favourable demographic trends are not in themselves sufficient to promote economic growth. Rather, a growing labour force combined with flexible labour markets, human capital investment and successful export promotion has generated employment (Lee and others, 1997).

Demographic change is also an important determinant of labour supply. In Europe, the working-age population is growing faster than total population which, accompanied by increasing female labour participation and weak employment generation, has produced persistently high unemployment. Another feature is the unprecedented withdrawal of older men from the workforce (see table 6 and fig. V). Declining participation is due, at least in part, to improved pension benefits and the easing of eligibility for claiming disability benefits and pensions.

TABLE 6. LABOUR FORCE PARTICIPATION RATES OF OLDER MEN AND WOMEN, MORE DEVELOPED AND LESS DEVELOPED REGIONS, 1995

	Ages		
	55-59	60-64	65 or above
More developed regions			
Males	76	44	13
Females	42	23	6
Less developed regions			
Males	86	69	43
Females	44	31	14

Source: Based on International Labour Office, *Estimates and Projections of the Economically Active Population, 1950-2010*, 4th ed. (Geneva, 1996).

22

Figure V. Labour force participation rates, 1960 to 1995,
men aged 60-64 years

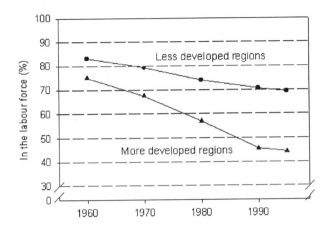

Source: International Labour Office, *Estimates and Projections of the Economically Active Population, 1950-2010*, 4th ed. (Geneva, 1996).

Sparked by the difficulty in sustaining pension systems, alternatives to the traditional pay-as-you-go schemes, in which current workers pay the benefits of current retirees, are being examined. These debates are framed against a broader context of redefining Governments' role in ensuring a minimum income for older persons, and have ushered in innovation and experimentation, particularly as concerns privatization. Faced with insolvency, some countries are bolstering the schemes' viability by raising the retirement age. In Latin America, countries are restructuring by adopting schemes that combine pay-as-you-go and privatized mandatory savings plans (United Nations/Economic Commission for Latin America and the Caribbean, 1997).

Changing age structure also poses challenges in the health and long-term care sector. These expenditures are concentrated among older populations, especially the oldest old. Spurred by the significant increase in the oldest old, expenditures for their care have risen dramatically, leading to the implementation of major reforms. Many of these measures aim for cost containment by expanding the number of nursing homes as an alternative to hospital-based services and by providing day care and respite care to enable older persons to remain in their own homes.

23

The convergence of demographic and other trends is resulting in smaller households. While gains in life expectancy imply a greater potential for co-residence, the percentage of older persons living with a child is rapidly decreasing in developed countries. In developing countries, the dominant living arrangement continues to be co-residence. With declining fertility and fewer caregivers, the tendency is one of weakening family support for older persons in developed and some developing countries, increasing strains on formal support. Most countries, especially in developing regions, rely almost exclusively on the extended family—usually women—to care for older persons. Working women are disadvantaged as they often have the triple responsibility of working, child-rearing and caregiving to ageing parents. Some countries are strengthening informal support by providing low-cost "granny flats" or according public housing priority to adults living with their parents.

Changes in age distribution have complex implications. An important issue is the allocation of limited public resources. Accordingly, planning requires sensitivity to demographic changes. As developed countries have shown, despite prolonged ageing, adjustment to ageing is not smooth. Given that large shifts in age structure are being compressed into a short period in developing countries, these countries will have less time than developed countries to adapt to changing age structure.

III. POPULATION DISTRIBUTION, URBANIZATION AND INTERNAL MIGRATION

A major transformation during the twentieth century has been the growth of urban centres and the concentration of population in urban areas. Throughout human history, the world has been primarily rural. However, this situation will change in the near future owing to the rapid growth of urban areas. As of mid-1998, 47 per cent of the world population lived in urban areas (see fig. VI). This urban population is growing three times faster than its rural counterpart. As a result, half of the world population is expected to be urban by 2006. Approximately three fifths of the world population will be living in urban areas by 2030 (United Nations, 1998d).

URBAN POPULATION GROWTH

In 1998, nearly two of every five persons lived in cities in the less developed regions, whereas about three of every four persons lived in cities in the more developed regions. This gap between the more developed regions and the less developed regions has narrowed since 1975. In 1975, 70 per cent of the population of the more developed regions was urban, while only 27 per cent of the population in the less developed regions was living in cities. The gap is expected to continue to narrow in the future, as rapid urbanization continues in the less developed regions. By 2030, it is projected that 57 per cent of the population in the less developed regions will be urban dwellers, about two thirds of the level in the more developed regions (84 per cent).

In 1998, 68 per cent of the world's urban population lived in the less developed regions. By 2030, 80 per cent will. This changing distribution of the world's urban population between the less developed and the more developed regions reflects the different rates of total population growth between these regions, as well as the different rates of urbanization. The urban growth rate of the world was 2.6 per cent annum during 1970-1990. It declined to 2.3 per cent per annum in 1995-2000, and it is expected to decline further to reach 1.6 per cent per annum by 2025-2030. In the less developed regions, the urban growth rate reached its peak at 3.8 per cent per annum during the 1975 to 1985 period, and has been declining since 1985. It is 3.2 per cent in 1995-2000, and is projected to decline to 1.9 per cent per annum between 2025 and 2030.

In spite of the declining rate of urban population growth, the average annual increment of the world's urban population is steadily becoming larger. While the annual increment during the period 1970-1998 was 50 million inhabitants, it is projected at 74 million between 1998 and 2030. Paralleling the shift of the world population from the more developed regions to the less developed regions, the latter are projected to account for an increasing share of the

Figure VI. Percentage of population residing in urban areas, 1970, 1998 and 2030

Source: Population Division, Department of Economic and Social Affairs of the United Nations Secretariat, *World Urbanization Prospects: The 1996 Revision* (United Nations publication, Sales No. E.98.XIII.6).

26

urban increment. Eighty-five per cent of the 50 million people added annually to the urban population during 1970-1998 is attributed to the less developed regions, and this share is further projected to reach 95 per cent from now until 2030, meaning that almost all urban dwellers adding to the world's population will be coming from developing countries.

The ratio of men to women is higher in urban areas than in rural areas in all regions of Africa (except for Northern Africa), as well as in Southern Asia and Western Asia, reflecting the predominance of males among migrants in cities. In Northern Africa, Eastern Asia and South-eastern Asia, the sex ratios are nearly the same in urban as in rural areas. In all the regions of Latin America and the Caribbean as well as in all the more developed regions, the ratios of men to women indicate that women tend to outnumber men among urban dwellers, partly because women tend to outnumber men in the migration streams directed to urban areas in those regions.

The proportion of urban dwellers living in agglomerations with 10 million or more inhabitants increased from 3 to 8 per cent between 1970 and 1995, and is expected to reach 11 per cent by 2015 (see fig. VII). These giant urban agglomerations, a relatively recent phenomenon in history, are becoming both larger and more numerous. In 1998, the largest cities in the world were Tokyo, with a population of 28 million, Mexico City (18 million) and São Paulo (17 million). By 2015, Lagos will be the third largest urban agglomeration in the world (25 million), after Tokyo (29 million) and Bombay (26 million).

Figure VII. Distribution of world urban population by city-size class, 1950, 1970, 1995 and 2015

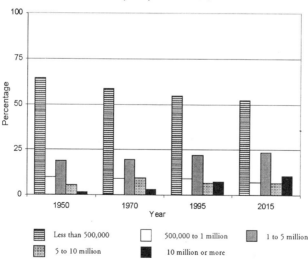

Source: Population Division, Department of Economic and Social Affairs of the United Nations Secretariat, *World Urbanization Prospects: The 1996 Revision* (United Nations publication, Sales No. E.98.XIII.6).

27

Between 1970 and 1998, the number of cities with 10 million or more inhabitants grew from 3 to 18. Of the 18 cities with 10 million or more inhabitants in 1998, 2 are in Africa (Lagos and Cairo), 4 in Latin America and the Caribbean, 2 in Northern America and 10 in Asia. It is projected that by 2015, 26 cities will have a population of 10 million or more (2 in Northern America, 2 in Africa, 18 in Asia and 4 in Latin America and the Caribbean). Despite the growing concentration of the urban population in large agglomerations, it is worth noting that half the world's urban population still live in smaller cities with less than 500,000 inhabitants.

The urbanization trends experienced by developed countries until the 1950s suggested that the increasing concentration of the urban population in ever larger urban centres was a natural concomitant of the rising proportion of people living in urban areas. However, between 1965 and 1985, a tendency towards population deconcentration was noticed in a number of developed countries. Berry (1976) coined the term "counterurbanization" to denote the process by which the larger metropolitan areas lost population, at least in relative terms, to smaller urban centres. Fielding (1982) provided a more rigorous definition of the term by suggesting that counterurbanization arises when there is a negative correlation between the net migration rate of places across the settlement system and their respective population. The widespread shift towards counterurbanization was first detected in the United States of America, where between the 1960s and 1970-1973 non-metropolitan areas passed from registering net migration losses of 300,000 persons annually to net gains of 400,000 annually (Beale, 1975). During the 1970s, the population in large metropolitan areas of the United States grew at half the rate of medium-sized and smaller metropolitan areas, with non-metropolitan areas outpacing the metropolitan aggregate (Frey, 1992). Other studies confirmed that similar developments were occurring in different developed countries, including Australia, Denmark, France, Germany, Italy, Japan, Norway and the United Kingdom of Great Britain and Northern Ireland, though the scale and timing of the phenomenon, and to some extent its nature, differed from country to country (Champion, 1989).

Despite the expectation that the shift away from population concentration in the larger metropolitan areas to that in medium-sized and small settlements would accelerate during the 1980s, recent evidence has failed to corroborate such a trend, and suggests that the tendency towards population concentration in the larger urban places has returned. The most significant reversal seems to have taken place in the United States during the 1980s, though there is also evidence that the growth rates of Paris, London and other agglomerations have increased in recent years (Champion, 1994; United Nations, 1995a).

Although the causes of both counterurbanization and the return of population concentration in larger metropolitan areas largely remain to be elucidated, several suggestions have been advanced (Champion, 1994). The fertility declines registered during the 1960s, which tended to be more accentuated in metropolitan areas, contributed to reducing the growth of those areas with respect to that of other urban centres. In addition, the growing levels of international migration, particularly during the late 1980s, coupled with the tendency of international migrants to settle in metropolitan areas, helped to accentuate the traditional form of population concentration. Yet changes in internal migration remain the key element leading to counterurbanization and its reversal. The underlying causes of those changes include the new spatial division of labour stemming from the changing structure of corporate organization that has made possible the relocation of manufacturing away from major industrial centres. The successful development of economic activity based in rural areas, particularly that associated with energy resource development, agriculture and forestry, was also a factor contributing to counterurbanization during the 1970s, especially in the United States. Changing residential preferences associated with changes in the age structure of the population appear to have played a role as well. Lastly, government actions regarding infrastructure investment, including the expansion of transportation networks and the improvement of health and educational services in smaller communities, the support provided for agriculture, forestry and rural development in general, and the adoption of decentralization policies and "new town" development all contributed to the fuelling of counterurbanization. However, the economic downturn that affected much of the developed world during the late 1970s and early 1980s weakened the commitment of Governments to those policies, and their subsequent deregulation of various elements of economic activity and service provision are likely to have renewed the advantages associated with the concentration of business, and consequently of population, in large metropolitan areas.

INTERNAL MIGRATION

Rural-to-urban migration is often viewed as the main cause of urban growth. However, the urban and rural populations of a country can change as a result of births, deaths, migration and areal reclassification resulting from changes of the boundaries defining urban and rural areas. Identifying the contribution of each of these components to urban and rural population change is fundamental for the study of the urbanization process, particularly in developing countries, where the pace of urban growth may pose serious challenges for those in charge of planning and formulating economic and social policy.

Estimates of the components of urban growth have been derived at the United Nations Population Division on the basis of information from consecutive censuses regarding the distribution of the population by place of residence (urban vs. rural), age group and sex. The components of urban growth were estimated for 36 developing countries in the 1960s, 41 in the 1970s and 27 in the 1980s.

Estimates of the proportion of urban growth attributable to net rural-urban migration and reclassification corroborate that, as concluded in an earlier study (United Nations, 1980), natural increase accounted for about 60 per cent of urban growth in the 1960s, whereas rural-urban migration accounted for the other 40 per cent. During the 1970s, there was a slight tendency for the contribution of rural-urban migration to increase (44 per cent), particularly because of its higher weight in Asia. But by the 1980s, when fertility had been reduced in many countries, net rural-urban migration accounted for 54 per cent of urban growth in developing countries, although its contribution varied by region, ranging from 25 per cent in Africa to 64 per cent in developing Asia (including China). Without China, net rural-urban migration accounted for about 50 per cent of population growth in the urban areas of other Asian countries. That is still a high proportion compared to the 34 per cent accounted for by migration in Latin America. These findings suggest that especially in regions characterized by economic stagnation, the role played by natural increase in explaining urban population growth has been strengthened.

The movement of people from rural to urban areas is only one of the possible forms of internal migration. In fact, despite the emphasis generally placed on it, rural-urban migration does not account for the largest proportion of internal migrants. In countries that are still largely rural, such as Ethiopia, India and Thailand, rural-rural migration is more important, whereas in countries that are highly urbanized, urban-urban migration dominates (as in Brunei Darussalam, the Republic of Korea in the 1990s, Brazil and Peru); that is to say, although rural-urban migration and its counterpart, urban-rural migration, contribute to the redistribution of population between urban and rural areas, at certain stages of the urbanization process the other types of migration (rural-rural and urban-urban) may be more important in the redistribution of population within each geographical stratum.

The participation of women varies by type of flow. In Egypt and India, for instance, women outnumber men in flows directed towards rural areas, especially in rural-rural migration. In contrast, in the Philippines, Thailand, Brazil and Honduras, women outnumber men in flows directed to urban areas, be they rural-urban or urban-urban. The participation of women in overall internal migration (without distinction as to type of flow) varies considerably from region to region. Among 15 countries with the required data, women accounted for at least 43 per cent of internal migrants in each of them and women outnumbered men among internal migrants in countries belonging to Latin America and the Caribbean. In addition, the share of women in internal migration in Cape Verde and Ethiopia was above 50 per cent, and in Nepal, Thailand and Zimbabwe it varied between 49 and 50 per cent.

GOVERNMENT VIEWS AND POLICIES

In 1998, 44 per cent of Governments considered their patterns of population distribution to be a major concern (see table 7). Another 29 per cent saw their patterns of population distribution to be a minor concern. In many developing countries, population distribution policies are largely synonymous with measures to reduce or even to attempt to reverse rural-urban migration, with the aim of controlling the growth of the primate city or other large metropolitan areas. Evidence indicates that these policies have not always been effective. Partly in response, many countries have adopted strong rural-oriented spatial policies.

Most African countries continue to be greatly concerned with reducing out-migration from rural areas. Thus, Africa has consistently been the region where Governments are most dissatisfied with their patterns of population distribution. In 1998, 63 per cent of the Governments in Africa considered their patterns of population distribution to be a major concern. Another 25 per cent saw population distribution as a minor concern. Only 12 per cent considered their patterns of population distribution to be satisfactory. Since the early 1960s, Asian countries have expressed strong dissatisfaction with patterns of population distribution. As of 1998, only 20 per cent of Asian countries considered their patterns of population distribution to be satisfactory, while 43 per cent viewed it as a major concern, and 37 per cent considered it to be a minor concern. The countries of Latin America and the Caribbean also considered their patterns of population distribution to be a concern. In 1998, just under half of countries in the region viewed population distribution as a major concern and 21 per cent viewed it as a minor concern. Europe has the highest proportion of Governments that consider their patterns of population distribution to be satisfactory—49 per cent in 1998. Thirty-one per cent of Governments report that they see population distribution as a major concern, while 20 per cent report it as a minor concern.

TABLE 7.   GOVERNMENTS' VIEWS ON SPATIAL DISTRIBUTION, 1998
(*Number of countries*)

	View			
By level of development	*Satisfactory*	*Minor change desired*	*Major change desired*	*Total*
World	49	52	78	179
More developed regions.	21	14	9	44
Less developed regions	28	38	69	135
Least developed countries . .	6	12	29	47

Source: Population policy data bank maintained by the Population Division, Department of Economic and Social Affairs of the United Nations Secretariat, *National Population Policies* (United Nations publication, Sales No. E.99.XIII.3).

Whereas many Governments throughout the developing world have strongly endorsed the concept of promoting small and medium-sized cities, how to go about it is far less clear. A number of Governments have also in recent years adopted policies that seek to work alongside market forces by channelling private investment to designated areas, providing infrastructure in underserved areas or removing subsidies that previously favoured the residents of certain locations, such as the national capital. The idea behind this approach is to create a "level playing field", whereby a number of areas of a country are equally attractive to potential migrants. Whereas there is continuing concern in many developing countries over the growth of giant cities, mega-city size per se may not always be a critical policy variable. The key challenge is to efficiently manage mega-city growth. Management of urban growth becomes more important as the integration of the world economy and the expansion of international trade and investment change the bases of urban economic growth in the twenty-first century.

31

IV. POPULATION GROWTH, ECONOMIC GROWTH, POVERTY, FOOD AND THE ENVIRONMENT

Discussions of the effects of population factors on development and the environment have been featured in numerous United Nations meetings and reports, including expert group meetings that were convened before each of the three United Nations intergovernmental conferences focusing on population and development concerns—the World Population Conference in 1974, the International Population Conference in 1984 and the International Conference on Population and Development in 1994 (see United Nations, 1973, 1975, 1991, 1994a, 1994b). There are many paths through which population factors could have either positive or negative effects on development. Empirically, it has been difficult to separate out the potentially offsetting effects of, for example, changes in birth rates and death rates and the implications of changing age structures, and it has also been difficult to isolate the effects of demographic factors from the many other contributors to economic and environmental change.

ECONOMIC GROWTH

Debates surrounding the consequences of population growth for the pace of economic development are both vigorous and contentious. Recent decades have witnessed major swings in thinking about population and development interrelationships. In general, the impacts of rapid population growth have been judged to vary considerably by country and over time, and have been considered to be relatively small by comparison with other determinants of economic prosperity. Nevertheless, there is a general view that the rapid population growth of many developing countries makes it more difficult for these countries to achieve improvements in their standard of living.

An influential study by the United States of America's National Research Council, in 1986, reached the qualitative conclusion that slower population growth would be beneficial to the economic development of developing countries (National Research Council, 1986). There are arguments to suggest that as fertility declines and the proportion of the population in the economically most productive ages rises, resources thereby freed from care for a larger child population can be productively directed to increased labour force participation (especially of women) and increased investment in both physical and human capital, thereby speeding economic development.

The importance of this effect was called into question, however, since more than a dozen studies using cross-country data for the 1960s and 1970s failed to unearth a statistically significant association between the growth rates of population and per capita output (Kelley and Schmidt, 1994). However, recent assessments have revealed fairly large, economically important negative correlations between population change and per capita output growth based on data for the 1980s or later and for the entire period from the 1960s through the early 1990s (United Nations, 1988; Kelley and Schmidt, 1998). The negative effect of high fertility on economic growth also appears greater for poorer countries.

Recent studies have gone beyond merely relating economic and population growth rates by examining separately different components or aspects of population change; these components can have effects that tend to cancel out when only the total rate of population growth is studied. The newer studies have focused especially on (*a*) age-distributional changes as emphasized in life-cycle modelling by economists, and (*b*) demographic components modelling (births, deaths, migrants) as emphasized by demographers and policy analysts (Kelley and Schmidt, 1995 and 1998; Bloom and Williamson, 1998). These decompositions reveal reasonably strong impacts of specific aspects of demographic change, even in cases where the overall effect of population growth appears nil. Such results show how a near-zero correlation between population and economic growth rates can conceal, during a historical period, important offsetting effects of the components of population change.

At present, this is an area of active research work, where models and results are still evolving. It is clear that the demographic factors remain important when other variables commonly employed to understand economic growth cross-nationally are included in the analysis. However, other questions remain to be answered, including how to reconcile the weak and inconsistent results for earlier periods with the strong results observed when more recent data are included. Has the impact of population growth changed? Is it that until recently few countries had progressed far enough through the fertility transition for the age-structural effects to become economically important? Could it be that the negative consequences of rapid population growth associated with diminishing returns to capital and the environment are emerging as relatively more important than, say, the positive impacts of scale, or induced innovation/technical change and/or attenuating feedbacks? Are there unique features associated with economic conditions in the 1980s (a period encompassing significant structural adjustments, world recession, wars and droughts) as well as the early 1990s (generally a period of stronger economic growth) that could account for the changed findings?

It is generally recognized that government policies condition the form and the size of population's impacts on the economy. Yet very little is known about how Governments react to rapid population growth, apart from policies aimed at influencing population growth itself. The Programme of Action of the International Conference on Population and Development reflected a consensus that slower population growth buys time for Governments to adjust. However, slowing population growth does not itself ensure that favourable policy and institutional changes will occur. The time bought by slower population growth may be squandered if needed policy changes are not made.

POVERTY

The general picture of poverty trends is mixed; some countries have en-
joyed impressive reductions (see table 8), while in sub-Saharan Africa, poverty
has remained high and persistent. Furthermore, the financial crisis that began in
Asia in 1997 has erased some of the gains. It is widely believed that the most
important factor accounting for poverty is the macroeconomic environment, especially factors that govern the growth of employment (Squire, 1993; Chen and
others, 1994; Lipton and Ravallion, 1993). To the extent that macroeconomic
growth is adversely influenced by the pace of demographic change, then poverty will be adversely impacted by rapid population growth as well. Statistical
studies of economy-wide data have not firmly established notable effects of
demographic change on poverty rates (Ahlburg, 1996; McNicoll, 1997;
Pritchett, 1997). However, a study employing recently compiled data for 45 developing countries found that high fertility contributes to greater poverty both
by retarding economic growth and by skewing the distribution of income
against the poor (Eastwood and Lipton, 1997).

TABLE 8. RECENT POVERTY TRENDS

Region	Number poor (millions)		Per cent of population below poverty level [a]	
	1987	1993	1987	1993
Developing and transition countries	1 227	1 314	30.1	29.4
Eastern Europe and Central Asia	2	15	0.6	3.5
Developing countries	1 225	1 299	33.3	31.8
Latin America and the Caribbean	91	110	22.0	23.5
Middle East and North Africa	10	11	4.7	4.1
Sub-Saharan Africa	180	219	38.5	39.1
South Asia	480	515	45.4	43.1
China, East Asia and the Pacific	464	446	28.2	26.0

[a]$1 per day in 1986 purchasing power parity prices.
Source: Division of Social Policy and Development, Department of Economic and Social Affairs of the United Nations Secretariat, Report on the World Social Situation, 1997 (United Nations
publication, Sales No. E.97.IV.1), p. 69.

It is often noted that high fertility may be a rational strategy of poor families in response to conditions of high mortality—high fertility is needed to ensure that some children will survive to adulthood—and to a traditional,
low-technology economy, in which (unschooled) children can begin to contribute economically at a relatively young age. However, for most of today's poor,
current conditions in the surrounding society are substantially different from
those of pre-modern times and are changing rapidly. The available evidence

from direct survey questions about family size desires suggests that in many settings, poor, rural and uneducated parents currently want only modestly larger families than their better-off counterparts. The actual difference in fertility levels between the more and less advantaged tends to be much larger than the difference in desired family size: apparently, the more advantaged groups have been more successful in achieving desired family size (United Nations, 1997b).

FOOD

Even though the expansion of food available per person in developing countries has grown at an impressive pace in recent decades (from 1,900 to 2,600 calories per day) and total food production has more than doubled, the distribution of food has been uneven, and starvation and malnutrition are still pervasive, especially in Africa and parts of Asia (Bender and Smith, 1997). In the face of notable demographic pressures in the future, a comparison of population with carrying-capacity estimates indicates that persistent food shortages can be avoided as long as there are improvements in and prudent management of rural sector production (Alexandratos, 1995; Bongaarts, 1996; Dyson, 1996; Smil, 1994). An important element in food provision is the need to reckon growing environmental costs. Deforestation constitutes the most conspicuous example of environmental change in farming. Studies across many countries and ecological settings reveal a positive correlation between deforestation and population growth (Bilsborrow, 1994; Birdsall, 1994; Palloni, 1992). The strength of these correlations varies substantially between settings and depends on such factors as access to and ownership of land, restrictions on foresting, the relative economic attractiveness of using intensive versus extensive cultivation techniques (strongly influenced by land tenure and government policies) etc.

ENVIRONMENT

Many Governments view their population size, growth or distribution as a cause for concern in relation to environmental problems (United Nations, 1997c). Water pollution, the amount of fresh water and deterioration of the urban environment are areas over which serious concern has often been expressed regarding population impacts. Rarely do Governments seek a solution to environmental problems solely through altering population trends or distribution. In many cases, though, Governments report a policy approach that combines measures to affect population trends or distribution with other approaches to alleviating environmental problems.

Given the nature of environmental resources, enlightened government policies are critical to population-environmental interactions. Because market and policy failures may be extensive, seemingly adverse impacts of population growth can be high, although slowing population growth may not halt environmental decay and the impacts in many settings may in reality be relatively small. This is because without government policies that correct market failures and provide appropriate incentives for individual/firm behaviours, environmental degradation will continue, albeit at a reduced pace, and the possibility of increased economic prosperity associated with reduced population growth can itself carry with it pressures on the environment. Thus, the impacts of demographic change can best be viewed as "amplifying" the impacts deriving from the more fundamental causes of environmental degradation.

SUMMARY

Poverty reduction, food provision and environmental maintenance are integrally linked with demographic, economic and political change. "Vicious circles" of cumulatively worsening performance in each of the latter two dimensions may be exacerbated by rapid population growth. Breaking this interacting web can be facilitated by government policies that promote income growth, empower the poor with education and health, and provide incentives to behave prudently in the allocation of resources. Such policies can lead to "virtuous circles" of cumulatively improving performance in all three dimensions. In such a situation, children are less likely to be seen as producing agents, women's and men's roles change, and the demand for reproductive health services increases. Economic and demographic change are mutually interacting forces influenced by institutional settings and government policy. As a result, population policies are an important element of the policy-making components needed to advance social and economic development, eliminate poverty and foster long-term environmental stewardship.

ANNEX
Data collection, data availability
and data quality

Knowledge of demographic change and its interrelationships with aspects of development needs to be based on timely and high-quality data. The principal data-collection systems for demographic and social information are population censuses, sample surveys and civil registration systems. These systems have provided the primary means for measuring basic demographic parameters, such as size and growth of population, components of growth and vital rates. Although international migration is an important source of demographic change, statistics on immigration and emigration are not available for many countries on a regular basis.

Population censuses remain the most important source of key demographic information at all geographical levels for the planning and implementation of development programmes. In the 1990 census decade, 202 countries and areas carried out their censuses, representing a 95 per cent coverage of the world's population (see table 9). The challenge countries are facing for the 2000 census round is how to mobilize resources to conduct future population censuses and look beyond the traditional sources of financing census activities by involving all sectors of civil society.

TABLE 9.   NUMBER OF COUNTRIES HAVING CONDUCTED A CENSUS DURING THE 1950, 1960, 1970, 1980 AND 1990 CENSUS DECADES, BY REGION

Census decades[a]	Total	Africa	North America	South America	Asia and Oceania	Europe
1985-1994	202	48	34	13	67	40
1975-1984	194	51	31	14	65	33
1965-1974	162	36	34	12	53	28
1955-1964	85	9	12	9	26	35
1945-1954	65	2	12	8	15	28

[a]The number of countries has increased over the years; as a result, the absolute change in additional number of countries participating in the census programmes may be somewhat distorted.

Sources: United Nations, *Demographic Yearbook*, 1963, 1964, 1983 and 1993 (United Nations publications, Sales Nos. E/F.64.XIII.1, E/F.65.XIII.1, E/F.84.XIII.3 and E/F.94.XIII.1); and Forest E. Linder, "World demographic data", in *The Study of Population* (University of Chicago Press, 1959).

Sample surveys are an important tool for obtaining detailed demographic and social data, particularly with respect to fertility and mortality. However, surveys normally cannot provide data at small geographical levels, and are therefore not a substitute for censuses. Nonetheless, because of their smaller scale, surveys have greater depth than a census, tend to employ better qualified and better trained enumerators than censuses do, and for fertility and mortality data are generally found to be relatively more reliable than the census.

When a complete and reliable civil registration system exists in a country, it is the ideal source of levels and patterns of fertility, mortality and nuptiality used to monitor population growth and assess the health situation of the population, including maternal, child and infant mortality for the country as a whole, and for its regions, subregions and communities. The main advantages of civil registration are its continuity, its permanency and its country-wide scope. Unfortunately, in many developing countries registration is either weak or almost entirely lacking.

Over the years, national statistical systems have improved considerably, but there is still much to be done to institutionalize those gains. Data-collection, processing and dissemination technologies are changing rapidly. Statistically less developed countries are lagging behind in respect of keeping pace with these rapid changes. In addition, data-collection costs are rising rapidly, and countries are finding it difficult to collect and disseminate data on a regular basis.

REFERENCES

Ahlburg, Dennis A. (1996). Population growth and poverty. In *The Impact of Population Growth on Well-being in Developing Countries*, D. A. Ahlburg and others, eds. Berlin: Springer-Verlag.

Alexandratos, Nikos, ed. (1995). *World Agriculture: Towards 2010: An FAO Study*. New York: John Wiley and Sons.

Asian Development Bank (1997). *Emerging Asia: Changes and Challenges*. Manila.

Beale, C. L. (1975). *The Revival of Population Growth in Non-Metropolitan America*. Washington, D.C.: Economic Research Service, United States Department of Agriculture.

Bender, William, and Margaret Smith (1997). Population, food, and nutrition. *Population Bulletin*, vol. 5, No. 4 (February).

Berry, B. J. L. (1976). The counterurbanization process: urban America since 1970. In *Urbanization and Counterurbanization*, B. J. L. Berry, ed. Beverly Hills, California: Sage.

Bilsborrow, Richard E. (1994). Population, development and deforestation. In Population, environment, development. In *Proceedings of the United Nations Expert Group Meeting on Population, Environment and Development, United Nations Headquarters, 20-24 January 1992*. Sales No. E.94.XIII.7. New York: United Nations.

Birdsall, Nancy (1994). Another look at population and global warming. In *Proceedings of the United Nations Expert Group Meeting on Population, Environment and Development, United Nations Headquarters, 20-24 January 1992*. Sales No. E.94.XIII.7. New York: United Nations.

_____ and Steven Sinding (1999). Draft report on a symposium on population change and economic development, 2-6 November 1998, Bellagio, Italy.

Bloom, David E., and Jeffrey G. Williamson (1998). Demographic transitions and economic miracles in emerging Asia. *World Bank Economic Review*, vol. 12, No. 3 (September).

Bongaarts, John (1996). Population pressure and the food supply system in the developing world. *Population and Development Review*, vol. 22, No. 3 (September).

Chackiel, Juan, and Susana Schkolnik (1997). Latin America: less advanced groups in demographic transition. Paper presented at the International Population Conference of the International Union for the Scientific Study of Population, Beijing, 11-17 October 1997.

Champion, Anthony G., ed. (1989). *Counterurbanization*. London: Edward Arnold.

Champion, Anthony G. (1994). Population distribution patterns in developed countries. In proceedings of the United Nations Expert Group Meeting on Population Distribution and Migration, Santa Cruz, Bolivia, 18-23 January 1993. ESA/P/WP.126.

Chen, Shaohua, and others (1994). Is poverty increasing in the developing world? *Review of Income and Wealth*, vol. 40, No. 4.

Cleland, John, and others (1994). *The Determinants of Reproductive Change in Bangladesh*. World Bank Regional and Sectoral Studies. Washington, D.C.: World Bank.

Dyson, Tim (1996). *Population and Food Production: Global Trends and Future Prospects*. New York: Routledge.

Eastwood, Robert, and Michael Lipton (1997). The impact of changes in human fertility on poverty. University of Sussex. Mimeograph.

Emmerij, Louis (1993). The international situation, economic development and employment. In *The Changing Course of International Migration*. Paris: Organisation for Economic Cooperation and Development.

39

Espenshade, Thomas, Leon F. Bouvier and Brian Arthur (1982). Immigration and the stable population model. *Demography*, vol. 19, No. 1.

Fielding, A. J. (1982). Counterurbanization in Western Europe. *Progress in Planning*, vol. 17, No. 1.

Frey, W. H. (1992). Perspectives on recent demographic change in metropolitan and non-metropolitan America. In *Population Change and the Future of Rural America*, D. L. Brown and L. Swanson, eds. Washington, D.C.: Economic Research Service, United States Department of Agriculture.

Golini, Antonio, Alessandra Righi and Corrado Bonifazi (1993). Population vitality and decline: the North-South contrasts. In *The Changing Course of International Migration*. Paris: Organisation for Economic Cooperation and Development.

International Labour Office (1996). *Estimates and Projections of the Economically Active Population, 1950-2010*, 4th ed. Geneva.

Kelley, Allen C., and Robert Schmidt (1994). *Population and Income Change: Recent Evidence*. World Bank Discussion Papers, No. 249. Washington, D.C.: World Bank.

_____ (1995). Aggregate population and economic growth correlations: the role of the components of demographic change. *Demography*, vol. 32, No. 4 (November).

_____ (1998). Economic and demographic change: a synthesis of models, findings and perspectives. Paper prepared for a symposium on population change and economic development, Bellagio, Italy, 2-6 November.

Keyfitz, Nathan (1971). Migration as a means of population control. *Population Studies*, vol. 25, No. 1.

Kirk, Dudley (1996). Demographic transition theory. *Population Studies*, vol. 50, No. 3 (November).

Lee, Ronald, and others (1997). *Saving, Wealth and the Demographic Transition in East Asia*. Working Paper, No. 88-7. Honolulu: East-West Center.

Linder, Forest E. (1959). *World Demographic Data*. In *The Study of Population*. University of Chicago Press.

Lipton, Michael, and Marin Ravallion (1993). *Poverty and policy*. World Bank Policy Research Department Working Paper, No. WPS 1130. Washington, D.C.: World Bank.

Mason, Karen Oppenheim (1992). Culture and the fertility transition: thoughts on theories of fertility decline. *Genus*, vol. XLVIII, No. 3-4 (December).

McNicoll, Geoffrey (1997). *Population and Poverty: A Review and Restatement*. Population Council Working Papers in Policy Research, No. 105. New York: Population Council.

National Research Council (1986). *Population Growth and Economic Development: Policy Questions*. Washington, D.C.: National Academy Press.

Palloni, A. (1992). *The Relation Between Population and Deforestation: Methods for Drawing Causal Inferences from Macro and Micro Studies*. University of Wisconsin (Madison) Center for Demography and Ecology Working Paper, No. 92-14.

Pritchett, Lant (1997). Review of Robert D. Kaplan's *The Ends of the Earth: From Togo to Turkmenistan, from Iran to Cambodia—a Journey to the Frontiers of Anarchy. Finance and Development* (March).

Qatar, Ministry of Health (1991). *Qatar Child Health Survey*. Abdul-Jalil Salman, Khalifa Al-Jaber and Samir Farid, eds. Doha, Qatar.

Smil, Vaclav (1994). How many people can the earth feed? *Population and Development Review*, vol. 20, No. 2.

Squire, Lyn (1993). Fighting poverty. *American Economic Review*, vol. 83, No. 2 (May).

United Arab Emirates, Ministry of Health (1991). *United Arab Emirates Child Health Survey*. Abdul-Wahab and others, eds. Abu Dhabi.

United Nations (1964). *Demographic Yearbook, 1963*. Vol. 15. Sales No. E/F.64.XIII.1.

_____ (1965). *Demographic Yearbook, 1964*. Vol. 16. Sales No. E/F.65.XIII.1.

_____ (1973). *The Determinants and Consequences of Population Trends*, Population Studies, No. 50. Sales No. E.71.XIII.5.

_____ (1975). *The Population Debate: Dimensions and Perspectives.* Papers of the World Population Conference, Bucharest, 1974. Vols. I and II. Population Studies, No. 57. Sales Nos. E/F/S.75.XIII.4 and E/F/S.75.XIII.5.

_____ (1980). *Patterns of Urban and Rural Population Growth.* Sales No. E.79.XIII.9.

_____ (1985). *Demographic Yearbook, 1983.* Vol. 35. Sales No. E/F.84.XIII.1.

_____ (1988). *World Population Trends and Policies: 1987 Monitoring Report.* Sales No. E.88.XIII.3.

_____ (1990). *Patterns of First Marriage: Timing and Prevalence.* ST/ESA/SER.R/111.

_____ (1991). *Consequences of Rapid Population Growth in Developing Countries. Proceedings of a United Nations/Institut national d'études démographiques expert group meeting, New York, 23-26 August 1988.* New York, Taylor and Francis.

_____ (1994a). *Population, Environment and Development: Proceedings of the United Nations Expert Group Meeting on Population, Environment and Development, United Nations Headquarters, 20-24 January 1992.* Sales No. E.94.XIII.7.

_____ (1994b). Pcpulation growth and demographic structure. Proceedings of the United Nations Expert Group Meeting on Population Growth and Demographic Structures, Paris, 16-20 November 1992. ESA/P/WP.128.

_____ (1995a). *World Urbanization Prospects: The 1994 Revision.* Sales No. E.95.XIII.12.

_____ (1995b). *Demographic Yearbook, 1993.* Vol. 45. Sales No. E/F.94.XIII.1.

_____ (1996). *Levels and Trends of Contraceptive Use as Assessed in 1994.* Sales No. E.96.XIII.13.

_____ (1997a). *Report on the World Social Situation, 1997.* Sales No. E.97.IV.1.

_____ (1997b). *World Population Monitoring, 1996: Selected Aspects of Reproductive Rights and Reproductive Health.* Sales No. E.97.XIII.5.

_____ (1997c). *Government Views on the Relationships Between Population and Environment.* Sales No. E.98.XIII.7.

_____ (1998a). World population monitoring, 1998: health and mortality, selected aspects. ESA/P/WP.142.

_____ (1998b). Summary report on an expert group meeting on below-replacement fertility, New York, 4-6 November 1997.

_____ (1998c). *World Population Projections to 2150.* Sales No. E.98.XIII.14.

_____ (1998d). *World Urbanization Prospects: The 1996 Revision.* Sales No. E.98.XIII.6.

_____ (1999a). *World Population Prospects: The 1998 Revision,* vol. I, *Comprehensive Tables.* Sales No. E.99.XIII.9.

_____ (1999b). *World Population Prospects: The 1998 Revision,* vol. II, *The Sex and Age Distribution of the World Populations.* Sales No. E.99.XIII.8.

_____ (1999c). *National Population Policies.* Sales No. E.99.XIII.3.

_____ /Economic Commission for Latin America and the Caribbean (1997). *Economic Survey of Latin America and the Caribbean, 1996-1997.* Sales No. E.97.II.G.2.

_____ /Joint United Nations Programme on HIV/AIDS (1999). The demographic impact of HIV/AIDS. Report on a technical meeting, New York. ESA/P/WP.152.

United Nations Children's Fund (1998). *The State of the World's Children, 1998.* New York: Oxford University Press.

World Health Organization (1998). *The World Health Report, 1998: Life in the Twenty-first Century: A Vision for ALL.* Geneva.

41

Litho in United Nations, New York
93274—November 1999—6,745
ISBN 92-1-151338-3

United Nations publication
Sales No. E.99.XIII.15
ST/ESA/SER.A/181

CONGO

Brazzaville —
● Centre d'Hygiène générale
● Hôpital militaire
● Laboratoire national
Loubomo —
Centre d'Hygiène générale
Pointe-Noire —
● Centre d'Hygiène générale
● Infirmerie de garnison

CUBA

Yellow-Fever Vaccinating Centre

Camagüey Province

Camagüey City
Nuevitas Port

Ciego de Avila Province

Ciego de Avila City

Cienfuegos Province

Cienfuegos Port

Granma Province

Bayamo City

Guantánamo Province

Guantánamo City

Havana Province

Alquizar International Motel
Mariel Port
Port — Havana City
Port — Pesquero de Havana

Holguín Province

Holguín City

Isla de la Juventud Province

Nueva Gerona City

Las Tunas Province

Las Tunas City

Matanzas Province

Matanzas Port

Pinar del Río Province

Pinar del Río City

Sancti Spíritus Province

Sancti Spíritus City

Santiago de Cuba Province

Santiago de Cuba City
Santiago de Cuba Port

Villa Clara Province

Santa Clara City

CYPRUS
CHYPRE

Nicosia —
General Hospital

CZECHOSLOVAKIA
TCHÉCOSLOVAQUIE

Bratislava —
Regional Hygiene Station — Krajská
hygienická stanice
Brno —
Regional Hygiene Station of South Mo-
ravia — Krajská hygienická stanice Jiho-
moravského kraje
České Budějovice —
Regional Hygiene Station of South
Bohemia — Krajská hygienická stanice
Jihočeského kraje
Hradec Králové —
Regional Hygiene Station of East
Bohemia — Krajská hygienická stanice
Východočeského kraje

CZECHOSLOVAKIA *(continued)*
TCHÉCOSLOVAQUIE *(suite)*

Ostrava —
  Regional Hygiene Station of North Moravia — Krajská hygienická stanice Severomoravského kraje
Plzeň —
  Regional Hygiene Station of West Bohemia — Krajská hygienická stanice Západočeského kraje
Praha (Prague) —
  • Hygiene Station of the Capital — Hygienická stanice hl. m. Prahy
  • Department of Sanitary Protection of State Frontier, Ruzyne Airport — Oddĕleni zdravotní ochrany státních hranic, Letištĕ Ruzynĕ
Ústí nad Labem —
  Regional Hygiene Station of North Bohemia — Krajská hygienická stanice Severočeského kraje

DEMOCRATIC KAMPUCHEA
KAMPUCHEA DÉMOCRATIQUE

Phnom Penh —
  Institut de Biologie

DEMOCRATIC YEMEN
YÉMEN DÉMOCRATIQUE

Aden —
  Port Health Officer, Tawahi
Little Aden —
  • B.P. Refinery Hospital
  • Port Health Services
Mukalla —
  Hospital
Saiun —
  Hospital

DENMARK
DANEMARK

Ålborg —
  Statens Seruminstitut

Århus —
  Statens Seruminstitut
Esbjerg —
  Dr Jorn Brix, Storegade/Ingemanns Alle
København (Copenhagen) —
  • Legekontoret, Danmarks Rederiforening
  • Statens Seruminstitut
Odense —
  Statens Seruminstitut
Rønne —
  Embedslaege Knud Simonsen, Embedslaegeinstitutionen for Bornholms amt, Ullasvej 13
Sønderborg —
  Mikrobiologisk afdeling, Sonderborg Sygehus
Vejle —
  Klinisk-microbiologisk afdeling, Vejle sygehus

DJIBOUTI

Djibouti —
  Service d'Hygiène et d'Epidémiologie

DOMINICA
DOMINIQUE

Roseau —
  Health Department

ECUADOR
ÉQUATEUR

Guayaquil —
  Departamento de Epidemiología
Quito —
  Departamento de Epidemiología

EGYPT
ÉGYPTE

Alexandria —
* Quarantine Section, Alexandria Port
* Vaccination Centre. Mustafa Kamel
  Army Headquarters
Al Shallal —
  Quarantine Office
Cairo —
* Al Manial Travellers' Vaccination
  Centre, Al Manial Health Centre
* Biological and Vaccine Production
  Laboratories, Dokki
* Ma'adi Travellers' Vaccination
  Centre, Ma'adi Health Centre
* Quarantine Section, Cairo Airport
* The Armed Forces Vaccination
  Centre, Abbassia No. 1 and No. 2
* Travellers' Vaccination Centre, Al
  Tahrir Complex
* Travellers' Vaccination Centre, Con-
  tinental, Opera Square *(for foreigners
  and diplomats — pour étrangers et
  diplomates)*
* Travellers' Vaccination Centre,
  Triumph Square, Heliopolis
Port Said —
  Quarantine Section
Safaga —
  Quarantine Office (Red Sea)
Suez —
  Quarantine Section

EL SALVADOR

San Salvador —
  Dirección General de Salud, Oficina de
  Vacunación

ETHIOPIA
ÉTHIOPIE

Yellow-Fever Vaccination Centre

Addis Ababa
Asmara
Assab
Dire Dawa
Massawa

FIJI
FIDJI

Lautoka —
  Health Office
Nadi —
  International Airport
Suva —
  Health Office

FINLAND
FINLANDE

Helsinski —
* National Public Health Institute
* Finnair Ltd. Medical Department
  (No. 224)
* Helsinki University Occupational
  Health Centre
Jyväskylä —
  Regional Public Health Institute
Kuopio —
  Regional Public Health Institute
Lappeenranta —
  Regional Public Health Institute
Mariehamn —
  Aland Municipal Health Centre
Niinisalo —
  Military Hospital
Oulu —
  Regional Public Health Institute
Rovaniemi —
  Regional Public Health Institute
Seinäjoki —
  Regional Public Health Institute
Turku —
  Regional Public Health Institute

Municipal Health Centre

Häme Province

Forssa
Hämeenlinna
Kangasala
Kartano
Lahti
Lammi
Lempäälä

18

FINLAND *(continued)*
FINLANDE *(suite)*

Mänttä
Nastola
Nokia
Orivesi as
Pirkkala
Riihimäki
Ruovesi
Somero
Tampere
Toijala
Turenki
Vääksy
Valkeakoski
Viiala
Virrat
Ylöjärvi

Keski—Suomi Province

Äänekoski
Jämsä
Joutsa
Jyväskylä
Keuruu
Laukaa
Muurame
Saarijärvi
Vaajakoski
Viitasaari

Kuopio Province

Iisalmi
Juankoski
Kiuruvesi
Kuopio
Lapinlahti
Leppävirta
Nilsiä
Pielavesi
Siilinjärvi
Sonkajärvi
Suonenjoki
Varkaus
Vehmersalmi

Kymi Province

Anjalankoski
Elimäki

Hamina
Imatra
Jaala
Joutseno
Karhula
Kausala
Kouvola
Kuusankoski
Lappeenranta
Nuijamaa
Parikkala
Pyhtää
Ruokolahti
Savitaipale
Simpele
Taaveti
Taipalsaari
Ylämaa

Lappland Province

Ivalo
Kemi
Kemijärvi
Kittilä
Kolari
Laurila
Muonio
Pelkosenniemi
Pello
Posio
Ranua
Rovaniemi
Rovaniemi mlk
Salla
Simo
Sodankylä
Tornio
Ylitornio

Mikkeli Province

Heinävesi
Heinola
Juva
Kangasniemi
Kerimäki
Mäntyharju
Mikkeli
Pieksämäki
Savonlinna
Sysmä